Dear Tiara,

I'm sending y[ou]
Wrote about saving money cause hey
we all need this advice! Haha.
It's a quick read & hopefully has a few
useful things in it ☺!
Want to wish you a Merry Christmas!
I miss you like crazy all the time.
I wish I could have sleepovers &
watch real house wives with you & Linda.
Hopefully I will be out on the west
coast soon! I miss you guys too
much!!

PS: Christmas in July??? Haha.

Merry Christmas to the whole
Pettinger fam! Their adopted
daughter misses them very much.

XOX Karine.

ACHIEVING
FINANCIAL
FITNESS

JEFF WACHMAN

ISBN: 978-1-4834-3516-9 (sc)
ISBN: 978-1-4834-3515-2 (e)

Library of Congress Control Number: 2015911682

Lulu Publishing Services rev. date: 08/05/2015

CONTENTS

INTRODUCTION

Achieving Financial Fitness is designed to prepare readers of all ages for the financial challenges they face in three distinct stages of life. Creating wealth, caring for wealth and using your wealth to create a lifestyle of your choosing. After all we only have one life to lead so why not make it a great one!

My hope is that you will find this book interesting, inspiring and informative. It is short and should be easy to read in one sitting and that is because I did not pad it with stories just to fill pages. My goal is to share with you the most important financial principals I have learned from my thirty years of experiences in the business, financial services and in life.

Throughout my life I have made education and learning a continuous life choice and I am proud to share the most important lessons that I have learned with you. Many of these lessons are counterintuitive meaning they are opposite to social norms or conventional thinking.

Imagine for example the game of golf. Swing left and the ball slices to the right, swing harder and you'll probably miss the ball completely!

I chose the fitness theme because I believe that there is a natural similarity between the skills an athlete must master to perform at the highest level, and the skills we must master to be successful financially. This book will highlight the comparisons.

Achieving Financial Fitness is part one of a three part series. All three parts will combine to complete the PILOT program. Pilot is an acronym for

Planning   Investments   Lifestyle   Ownership   Time

When all five parts are combined in the proper proportions, they become a process that can lead to a lifestyle that is both fulfilling and rewarding.

In creating the PILOT program, my goal in working with my clients is to see them through to their chosen lifestyle.

Stage two, "Financial Fitness for Life" will focus on the planning, investing and time components of financial fitness.

Stage three, "Financially Fit for First Class" is about having the financial resources in place to provide the income and time you will need to enjoy a lifestyle that lets you do what you want, when you want.

You will no longer fly the plane; you will become a first class passenger on your flight through life.

(for more information on the PILOT program please visit my website. www. wachmanwealth.com)

To provide you with some background on me, I graduated from McGill University with a degree in business, majoring in economics and finance in 1980. However like many young people, I had such a variety of interests that an obvious direction for my career was not obvious to me! Parental direction added to this confusion, all of it based on good intentions of course, but not necessarily factoring in the skills and interests that would make me passionate about what I could do in my life over the long term.

What I have learned, as I expect many of us have, is that it is more fun and certainly more rewarding to be passionate about what you do in life and learn how to transform that passion into an earned living than to simply earn a living and save passion for other things. But keep in mind sometimes work has to be done that you don't love (like chores) so that a passionate goal can be achieved!

So I was effectively at a loss when it came to finding my first job but I did have one grand dream—and I wrote it down in a little black book (no, really)! I wanted to be financially independent by age 45, and I was 20 at the time. In my mind, financial independence did not mean *rich*. It meant that I would have the financial resources to do what I wanted to do when I wanted to do it. The dream was driven by a passion to be in control of my life and happy with the choices I could make. The skills I had to work with were a university degree a family with a strong entrepreneurial background and a healthy appetite for knowledge and experiences.

Life, as we all know, can send you in directions that you may not like and can challenge your determination and resolve. In my case I did not initially follow my natural skills and passions. My first job (working in the family business) was filled with employment challenges and stresses (nature's equivalent of a hurricane) that rocked my resolve and my world. The positive side of this experience was that I gained exposure to the realities of business that I would never have had in a non-family business, and I did learn many new skills and many lessons.

One lesson I had to learn the hard way was how to say no more often. In fairness to myself and to those of us with the same trait, I also learned that it is hard to say no when most experiences are new and one is curious to explore all of life's grandness.

Through the years, I discovered that many careers in life are burdened with major challenges. Farmers are challenged by weather, pests and crop prices; athletes are challenged by injury and health issues (some even by drug testing); and financial markets can challenge us with economic, political and financial storms.

The key question here is how do we react to these challenges?

Can we learn from them, try to stay realistic, remain optimistic and perhaps course correct when required?

When we have failed can we pick ourselves up, seek help or guidance and ultimately learn or change? Or, do we let the negatives experiences overpower us and force us to give up?

I have friends who were driven to despair or depression by frustrations in their life, work or relationships. This is when their character traits became most apparent; optimist versus pessimist, those who sought help and guidance Vs those who sulked, those who were able to learn from their experiences and those who could not.

This book is surely intended for those who want to learn about life and direct their futures.

One gem of insight I wish I had discovered early on is the existence of four simple rules that I think have universal application. I consider them rules of the universe (the "hitchhiker's guide" version, if you have read the Douglas Adams book) to leading a successful and rewarding life. I encourage you list them—in your own handwriting, on your IPad in a notebook or on the space provided in the back of this book. You must learn them by heart if they are to be effective.

If only I had discovered them when I was 20!

I wish you well on your journey through life, and if you are of the age that your journey has been a long and fruitful one, I hope you can share what you have learned for the benefit of those who are genuinely looking to find their way.

The Four Universal Rules for Success

As a young person, I often wondered if I would or even could be successful in life. What would it take? Did I have to be ruthless, selfish and totally self-absorbed to become successful? Was there something I could learn or study that would help me find my way?

Later in life I was introduced to a very simple but powerful rule system that, if followed, would lead to a rewarding and successful life. If I told you that mastering these four simple rules would be essential to achieving one's goals in life, would you believe me?

Consider, if you will, that I believe these rules have been informally refined over generations. They most likely have been handed down from successful families to their offspring and taught by example, not formally. Whenever I see someone who struggles to find his or her place in the world, I compare that person's lifestyle to the four rules I am about to share with you.

In almost every comparison, I have observed that when a rule was broken over time, it led to personal setbacks and frustration.

In the same way that successful businesses pass their business skills, experience and philosophy down to their successors, I believe successful families pass these four rules down to their children mostly by example. Doesn't this make sense?

So if your children are wondering what it will take for them to be successful in life, consider sharing these four fundamental rules with them.

1. Do what you say you will do.
2. Finish what you start.
3. Be on time.
4. Show your appreciation.

I believe that living by these four simple rules can virtually guarantee your success in life. In fact not living by these rules will reduce your success by about 25 percent per rule.

Take a moment to relate these rules to someone you know well. Is this person successful and generally happy? Compare his or her behaviour to each of the rules I've shared with you. Can you see a weakness that limits this person's success in the world?

I can bet the most successful people you know will have personality traits that exemplify at least three of these four rules.

Add a financial life coach, and your progress will accelerate dramatically.

CHAPTER ONE

Why financial fitness?

The vast majority of us never become all-star athletes. Indeed, the numbers are staggering: fewer than one in 100,000 hockey players will ever step onto the ice for an NHL team.[1] Fewer than one in 150,000 basketball players will ever shoot hoops—even for a day—in the NBA. Chances are equally daunting for baseball, soccer and football—and the odds become even steeper for individual sports like tennis, cycling and golf.

In some instances this can be due to physical limitations. A given individual may simply lack the speed, stature or innate ability to excel. Not everyone can be a Tiger Woods, Sidney Crosby, Roger Federer or Hailey Wickenheiser

But more often than not the real issue is not physical. Most potential athletes drop away from their sport at a relatively young age due to a

---

[1] Put another way, only 0.05 percent of kids from Ontario who start hockey will end up in the NHL. Currently, Ontario has the highest percentage of active NHL players (*National Post*, January 13, 2013).

combination of poor coaching, distraction and an inability to envision future success.

On the other hand, some athletes with no apparent innate physical attributes—or those even with substandard physiques—persevere and even achieve greatness. Think of individuals like NFL star quarterback Russell Wilson, former NHL star winger Theo Fluery and all-star Red Sox second baseman Dustin Pedroia. Each was told he would never make it. Yet each did—spectacularly.

So what separates successful athletes from the others?

It comes down to three things: staying focused, having a plan and a vision of the future and having the right team to guide you to your goal.

Achieving financial fitness is best played as a "team sport". It requires individual skills for sure, but the combined skills of the team that surrounds you, be they teammates or coaches and trainers, all working in harmony are required to truly be successful. In this respect, the game is mastered like many other sports that at first glance seem individualistic. Competitive cycling is an unusual example. At first glance one would think that it is the individual rider that will take the race because each day one rider is celebrated for winning that stage of the race. The overall leader gets to wear the yellow jersey, and at the end of the multi-day event an individual winner is crowned.

But the reality is much different in that the ability for one rider to do well over long distances in cycling is a function of their ability to build a team and to work together as a group. This can be as formal as an organized team in a big international event or, in the case of local or regional races, as individuals working out strategies informally with others as the race evolves.

If you observe a bike race, there is often a cluster of riders in a pack, known as a *peloton*. They form an integrated unit very similar to geese flying in formation, and they are made up of riders from all teams. The effect of the peloton is to shield a significant number of riders from the wind, allowing them to travel faster and with less effort than if they were riding alone. Even the lead rider in the peloton benefits from this drafting effect as the cyclist in back reduces drag from the tail end of the lead bike. This tactic is an essential part of a cycling race and requires tremendous skill and strategy to move individual team riders into position within the peloton; this must be done at the right time to compete for the sprint to the finish line.

When this tactic is carried out well, everyone benefits. Not only do chasers gain an advantage, but the synergy can allow all riders to achieve personal bests.

Chances are you may not be planning to become a professional cyclist or athlete. There is probably not a yellow jersey, Stanley Cup or World Series ring in your future. But you *are* going to have a future, and probably one much longer than you thought.

A lot of what that future can be will depend on how you approach things today. If you can apply the same principles that have made elite athletes successful to your own situation you will significantly improve your chances of success and you can do all that without ever breaking a sweat!

This book will provide you with some key insights in terms of managing—and growing—your financial wealth. It will take you through the stages of wealth accumulation from rookie, to veteran to all-star. It will help you think through the process of selecting the right financial advice, guidance and mentorship.

Just as it is true for outstanding athletes, staying focused, having a plan and vision for the future, and having the right coaches are essential to achieving financial fitness.

So let's explore why it is so important to envision a lifestyle that you want to create and maintain.

CHAPTER TWO

Who invented "retirement"?

The concept of planned financial security into old age is a relatively new one. The reason is pretty straightforward—the vast majority of people through the centuries simply did not live to old age.

This does not mean that some people didn't save. Charles Dickens gave us the mid-19th century example of Ebenezer Scrooge, who saved to a fault.

But if your life expectancy was say 50, you were probably expected to work right up until you died, and if you did happen to live longer, people expected family members or the church to look after you.

Then German's first chancellor, Otto von Bismarck, came along. Bismarck had a problem. He was an archconservative in a time of rising socialism. He needed a way to show that his government cared for the poor and the elderly. The solution was the introduction of the world's first government social security system—an old-age pension scheme—in 1889.

Bismarck, ever fiscally prudent, originally set the age of retirement at 70 knowing that practically no Germans could possibly reach that age!

Even when the eligible age was lowered by the government to 65 in 1916, fewer than two in 10 (20%) could expect to collect. The German plan became the model for the world. The United States launched their social security plan in 1935 and adopted the age-65 criterion. Canada and many other nations soon followed suit.

Over time, companies also created private pension plans, typically called defined benefits plans, with payouts that would start at age 65. Again, and for many years, only a relatively small number of employees benefited for more than a few years.

Now, fast-forward to the present. The most recent statistics tell us the average life expectancy in Canada is 80.93 years—and higher if you're female. Most corporate pension plans with defined benefits were based on a formula combining annual income with numbers of years worked, but they have become as rare as Toronto Maple Leaf Stanley Cup victories!

These plans placed the obligation to fund employee retirement on the company. With our modern economy, restructuring and lack of job security means the workforce is constantly in transition. Companies do not want the burden of responsibility to fund a pension plan for their employees who may have a very lengthy retirement. Today we generally have to save for our own pension, placing this responsibility on us. Add to this that unlike your grandfather's generation you are probably looking at a good 20 years of retirement or more—Statistics Canada projects that by 2031 the average life expectancy of Canadian males will be 81.6 years and a whopping 86.0 years for Canadian females.

This is not what the German chancellor—or the other architects of social security and old-age pension schemes—had to factor in when they designed their plans.

This is, of course, in most respects good news. Most of us want to live longer, especially if we have our health and the financial resources to enjoy life. But that's the rub. If you're going to spend 20 to 40 years in retirement, you'd better have thought this through and set aside a fair amount of personal wealth to maintain a good quality of life for what could be a very long time.

The numbers are big. For example, if we can assume a rate of return of 5 percent on your savings, you would need $800,000 to generate $40,000 a year to live on (before factoring in inflation and tax). Not a trivial amount of money.

Are you anticipating an inheritance? The reality is that most parents are not planning to leave their children a ton of cash. They want to enjoy life in retirement—and they're living longer, so there may not be much left over to inherit.

So at the end of the day, the ball is squarely in your court. As with any big challenge, in sports or in the world of personal finance, it helps to break the problem down into smaller, more manageable components. It is also almost always better to tackle the challenge earlier rather than later. The next chapter will put things into context, especially if you are a member of the millennial generation.

Authors William Strauss and Neil Howe wrote about the Millennials in *Generations: The History of America's Future, 1584 to 2069*, Several alternative names have been proposed by various people: *Generation We*, *Global Generation*, *Generation Next* and the *Net Generation*. Millennials are sometimes also called Echo Boomers, referring to the generation's size relative to the Baby Boomer generation and due to the significant increase in birth rates during the 1980s and into the 1990s. In the United States, birth rates peaked in August 1990 and a 20th-century trend toward smaller families in developed countries continued.

CHAPTER THREE

The Millennials

If you were born between 1980 and 2000, you are generally considered to be part of the millennial generation, also sometimes referred to as generation Y. Research indicates you are tech savvy, independent and somewhat sceptical*, but with a strong sense of community and social obligation.

*The actual definition in Oxford English dictionary of sceptical is:

"Not easily convinced; having doubts or reservations."

It is not necessarily negative or pessimistic which is how many people view the term!

Much like the Greatest Generation (generally those born between 1901 and 1924), whose outlook was shaped by the Great Depression and World War II, millennials have lived through a period of economic shock, in the form of the Economic Crisis of 2008, as well as the trauma of 9/11 and a subsequent period of nearly continuous conflict in places like Afghanistan, Iraq and Syria. Many were forced to delay entry into the workforce because of poor job opportunities, and once there, they found advancement prospects initially not good.

The good news is that this picture is beginning to change. The world economy is improving. Baby boomers who may have put off retirement because of the economic crisis are now moving into their retirement years and jobs are opening up as they retire. Young people are finding more appropriate jobs and opportunities. Some are literally emerging from their parents' basements into the light of increased opportunity.

Those who have seen their parents struggle through numerous economic and financial crises may be discouraged from saving in a structured way because they fear for their savings or are simply discouraged by the entire industry. If this is the case, let's challenge these perceptions.

This is important. Today there are approximately 85 million millennial's in the United States and about nine million in Canada. By 2020 they will make up more than half the workforce in both countries. History, and basic math, has shown that the ideal time to ensure long-term economic security is when you are young.

That's why using athletes, as examples is so powerful. Athletes have to take action when they are young. Their window of opportunity is relatively short compared to the rest of us. But the lessons we can learn from them can be applied to financial challenges at all ages and all stages in life.

So now lets think of ourselves as elite athletes and lets pilot our progress from rookie to veteran to all star with our financial fitness in mind.

CHAPTER FOUR

The Rookie

Whether you're a young professional athlete or a green employee, you're a rookie. Rookies are great—so full of promise and potential. However, be it on the rink, soccer field or in the workplace, rookies are prone to making mistakes. Often, even the most talented stumble and their stumbles are called "rookie mistakes" but they are largely forgiven on the assumption that time and experience will rapidly improve their "game".

In this chapter I hope to outline the best financial practices with the goal of reducing or eliminating rookie financial mistakes. Avoiding early career errors can have big consequences down the line, often by making the difference between becoming an All-Star or an underperformer.

The sports analogy works well in this chapter. Prior to 1975, most professional athletes in North America either represented themselves or had their father represent them in contract negotiations. They also typically had a family member or friend handle their finances. Some did it themselves.

The results were often quite tragic. Leigh Steinberg, a sports agent and attorney who served as the model for the title character in the film *Jerry Maguire*, paints a sad picture of life for athletes in the days before athletes had professional representation.

Writing in *Forbes* magazine, he notes that the first instinct of a young athlete is to "buy big"—a big and expensive car, a big and expensive house and a big and sometimes very expensive lifestyle, For the rookie in the workplace, you might substitute a new car and a two-bedroom condo for an athlete's Ferrari and 4,000 sq. ft. villa, but the analogy is obvious.

When Steinberg began his career back in 1975 he negotiated an industry shaking multi-year, multimillion dollar contract for quarterback Steve Bartkowski when most professional athletes could barely afford to buy a VW Beetle, much less a Ferrari.

The average salary for an NFL player in the mid-1970s was $30,000, and players played for an average of 4.1 years. Baseball, hockey and basketball numbers were very similar. In individual sports like tennis and golf, only the elite few made much above those salary levels.

In 2014, thanks in large part to TV rights and professional representation, the average NFL salary grew to $2.2 million; the average MLB salary, $3.4 million and the average NHL salary, $1.3 million.

Of course, according to Steinberg, "all a top sports agent can do is *get* you the money. Financial planners are the ones to help you *keep* and *grow* the money."

Steinberg believes that a good sports agent and a good financial planner ask essentially the same questions.

To get an athlete to be introspective and evaluate their own goals and priorities, as an agent I ask them four basic questions:

1) What are your long-term financial goals?
2) What do you wish for your family?
3) Where do you want to play?
4) Where do you want to live when you retire?

According to Steinberg, the point of the questions is to get the athlete to project themselves into the future, to have specific goals and to build a plan to achieve those goals. The good news for athletes is that they will often have a significant signing bonus of money right from the start. The bad news is that their time frame is often very short. Even the most talented and fit athletes will likely have a career that ends by age 40, if not earlier.

Knowing this, we still read stories that can break your heart. In the *Sports Illustrated* article "How Athletes Go Broke," former Notre Dame star running back Rocket Ismail, who signed an $18.2 million four-year contract in 1991 with the CFL Toronto Argonauts, relates how he managed to essentially "lose it all." "After year one, which I had started with $4 million, I looked at my bank statement and I just went, 'What the ...!'" Ismail recalls. He had not only given in to what financial experts call "the lure of the tangible"—fancy cars, clothes and living arrangements—he had also begun making what became a string of high-risk investments in everything from a start-up restaurant (80 percent fail in the first year), to movies (which make restaurants look like a safe investment) to a record label (just as records were starting to disappear).

The end result? Rocket Ismael went bankrupt and he wasn't alone.

Just two years after retirement, *78 percent of former NFL players have declared bankruptcy.* Within five years of retirement, 60 percent of NBA players have done the same.

These statistics are unbelievable. How can someone earning more than the average person earns in a lifetime go broke in five years? This clearly illustrates the emotional forces that are at work within us challenging our every decision.

The demon and the saint one egging us on to do something NOW the other perhaps begging us to consider the long term effects before acting!

Fortunately, while no one is likely to give you an $18.2 million dollar four-year contract when you take your first job, you are very likely to be employed for twice or even three times as long as a professional athlete. Time, you will find, can be your friend. But in one respect you are exactly like that athlete. You are a rookie in the "National Financial League" and you need to decide what to do with your first paycheque.

Your temptation may be the same as Rocket Ismail—to succumb to the lure of the wealthy. A newer car; a more expensive apartment; an exotic vacation—all of these will tempt you. This is why, even before that first paycheque is deposited or electronically transferred into your bank account, you need goals, a plan and coaches to help you achieve them.

Like most hockey players, Wayne Gretzky probably started out at a very young age saying, "I want to win the Stanley Cup." After all, no one starts out by saying, "Someday I want to lose a Stanley Cup final."

What separates the Gretzkys and Nashes from the rest of us (aside from talent) is that they (often supported by a coach or mentor) envision all the steps they need to take, all the training and preparation work and practice time. In short, all of the individual stepping-stones needed to achieve their ultimate goal.

Everyone's goals are personal. It does not matter *what* they are as long as they are important to you. They could be as diverse as owning a house, starting a business or travelling the world, or they could be relevant to your family, relationships, finances or education.

Some goals—like happiness and spiritual contentment—may not require much in the way of money. (Although, as Mae West once said, "Too much of a good thing can be wonderful!") But if your goals are of a type that require financial strength or financial independence as a prerequisite, then a lifestyle that maximizes your savings right from the start will be the quickest way to achieve them.

Using the same methods required to train for an Olympic sport, you will need destination, visualization, discipline and focus. Some of your friends may not understand your goals or share your strategy. They may tempt you to splurge on everything from your first apartment rental to travel and luxuries. But what your friends might consider behaviour that is un-cool or overly frugal will not feel that way to you at all. *In fact, by taking control of your goals, you will feel empowered because you can see yourself moving toward the very future you have envisioned.*

It is the same as the feeling you get when you've finish a really tough workout or challenge yourself to run further, ride harder, swim faster. Yes, there is pain and you sometimes have to play a mind game with yourself to stay the course. But when you reach your goal you'll know what it takes and the next time you challenge yourself the actions you need to take to meet the challenge will seem natural and the results even more rewarding.

So, financially speaking, how do you get yourself into a position of financial fitness?

The 30/30/40 Formula

One rule my dear friend Steve Benjamin has used and teaches is what he calls the 30/30/40 formula. In fact, I am suggesting that this formula is almost a guaranteed formula for financial fitness. It is actually a ratio that, when followed, can allow you to accumulate cash *fast*. One of the biggest challenges for a new "financial athlete" is to have the resources to make investments without resorting to expensive debt.

This is how it works. Right out of the gate, with your first job, fully 30 percent of your income should be set aside for savings. The next 20-30 percent will go to taxes and the remaining 40 percent can be allocated to living expenses.

How does this translate into dollars?

Let's say your first job out of university pays you $60,000.

- $16-18,000 (approximately) will go to taxes
- $18-20,000 to savings
- And just $24,000 will be left for living expenses.

Can you find a way to live on $2000/month? If you can, you will save (with modest growth) close to $20,000 a year. This could mean having enough money to buy a car (for cash) in 18 months. Save for two years and have a down payment on a rental property or a condo—all while your friends may have partied their salary away.

Do this for five years and you are looking at $100,000—enough to start your own business or help finance whatever goal you set out to achieve. After two years your friends may be living the same way they are living now—but with nothing to show for it, while you will have assets that appreciate. The secret is in knowing that committing to this formula now will allow you to achieve your financial goals faster than anyone around you. You will accelerate your performance to a level that can move you into the top tier of financial athletes. As a result of your determination, commitment and training, your financial wealth and opportunities will grow exponentially.

The critical variable in all of this is time. Every year—every month that you delay is time lost forever. Your life's timeline is finite. Each year of opportunity ignored means the loss of many multiples of savings and growth. If your ultimate goal is financial freedom at the All-Star stage, you need to get started on the right foot as a rookie.

You may be thinking, how can I possibly live on 40 percent of my take-home pay? Well, if you were a student prior to obtaining your first job, you were probably living on that—or less. This one strategy means you just keep living like a student for a little while. That might mean getting an apartment with a couple of roommates or continuing to live in your parents' house for a time (perhaps paying some rent). It might also mean continuing to use public transport or putting off some more expensive purchases for a short time, but the payoff down the road will compound your efforts into something truly massive, something akin to moving from a fourth-line player to a second- or first-line player—more ice time, better income and more control of your life!

As mentioned earlier, some call this deferred or delayed gratification—but that's not really true because your *real* gratification will come through knowing that your financial training is paying off. You are getting financially stronger. Fitter athletes can do more and have better options. This strategy will set up a positive feedback loop that means achieving one's goals sooner—and that will be more than gratifying; *it is, in fact, addictive!*

Let's use another example to illustrate this same process and include the passage of time and the effects of compounding interest on your savings.

This time imagine you are 25 years old and your grandmother has left you and your twin brother each an inheritance of $100,000. You, being the visionary twin, are the ambitious one. You decide to meet with your parents' financial planner to discuss your financial options.

At your first meeting your planner draws up a diagram that looks like this:

Compounding Chart for 10 Year Increments					
Age	**25**	**35**	**45**	**55**	**65**
Assets	**100k**	**200k**	**400k**	**800k**	**1.6m**

This is a classic compounding chart that illustrates the value of investments over 10-year increments. In this example, the long-term rate of growth is just over

seven percent per year.

Your twin brother, on the other hand, has other ideas. He indulges in cars and travel and only *at age of 35* does he realize that he has spent all his savings on assets **that cost him money to maintain or that depreciate in value each year.**

When you get together over dinner on the 10th anniversary of your inheritance, you compare financials. Your twin brother learns that your inheritance has now grown to about $200,000. He on the other hand has squandered his inheritance and has little to show for it.

So, frustrated with his decisions, soon after your dinner your twin decides to save as much as he can, which based on his income stream and family situation allows him to save about $10,000 a year.

Under this scenario, it will take him up to 10 years—until the age of 45—to save the $100,000 you both started with at age 25, and by age 65 he will have saved a total of $300K (this is principal only and does not include growth or interest).

With compounded growth at about 7 percent, his diagram and numbers could look something like this:

7% Componded Growth				
Age	35	45	55	65
Assets	0	103k	309k	721k

Comparing your initial investment of $100K and **no additional savings** with compounded growth, by age 65 your chart will look like this:

With 100K Initial Investment				
Age	35	45	55	65
Assets	210k	414k	814k	1.6m

You could have close to $1.6m on an initial investment of $100,000 versus your brother, who has only $720k on an investment of $300k.

Starting to get the concept? Think of how your lifestyle could improve with the extra $10K your brother has to save that you have available to spend (or save).

Consider the effect in this simple example of continuing to save as your income grows each year. By saving—and investing—early and allowing your money to compound for those 10 years, you could have done everything your brother did with his $100K (only doing this over a 10-year period) and end up with well over a million dollars at age 65. Any way you look at it, it is an all star strategy!

CHAPTER FIVE

Borrowing to Invest

The idea of borrowing money to invest in your future growth can make sense if you approach this strategy with caution and follow some important rules.

If you were an All Star financial athlete, looking back on your investments with the benefit of experience, you probably would feel that you should have borrowed to invest more and sooner! The fact is that for most financial rookies, their first time borrowing to invest in a purchase is their home. Generally over time this works out to be a very good use of borrowed money This in spite of the fact that houses average rate of appreciation are about the rate of inflation 2-3%, and that there are many costs associated with owning a house like taxes and maintenance.

I would consider a house forced savings that over time allows us to keep some of the rent money we would have otherwise transferred to another home-owner namely a landlord.

An additional advantage of borrowing to invest is that the interest and management fees you pay are tax deductible.

Borrowing to Invest (these rules are intended for investment portfolios)

The Rules That Must Be Followed

1) Best done at an early age.
2) Interest rates must be low.
3) Investments must be well-diversified and tax-efficient.
4) Time frame must be longer than 10 years.

Lets take as an example a financial rookie age 25, who instead of saving $800/month in a savings account borrows to invest.

Initial amount borrowed $100k

Average rate of interest 5 percent

The estimated rate of return 7 percent (avg)

For tax purposes, interest on loan is tax deductible at 40 percent

Let's assume you never repay the original loan until age 65.

Not bad considering your twin brother's result of saving $10,000 per year for ten years. To reach $721K by age 65.

Age	25	35	45	55	65
Investment Growth	100k	200k	400k	800k	1.6 m
Net costs (after interest and tax deductions)	0	(30k)	(60k)	(90k)	(120k)
Original loan repayment					(100k)
Net savings					1.38 m

In reality you will likely need some help to set all of this in motion. You will need proper guidance to structure your investments for the long term, a good relationship with a bank that is making the loan and proper loan arrangements.

You will also need a steady hand to guide you when markets get challenging.

Yes, a few athletes today are self-trained, but most realise they can achieve much more with the guidance and support of a good coach. And just as an athlete can struggle through periods of poor performance or injuries and recover, so can you and your retirement plan with the help of your financial coaching team!

The same is true when your goal is to achieve financial fitness.

Okay, so you've got me interested, you're saying. How do I start to train?

Your first step should be to find a proven coach. If your goals are financial, then your first and most important coach will be a financial fitness coach.

One decision you will need to consider is whether or not to select someone who charges for the service provided, much as a personal trainer or a golf pro.

Do not be hesitant to pay a professional if he or she can provide a truly personalized coaching program that sets out the steps you will need to take. After all, these are certified professionals who have resources and contacts to assist you in every area of your financial life, and this, above all, is what you will need to achieve your financial goals faster.

What does it cost? Financial planning fees can start at $2,500 for your initial plan and can have an annual fee charged to your investments, negotiated flat rate or hourly.

The financial industry makes claims that there are many sources of financial expertise, from a bank employee to an insurance agent and a financial advisor, but in my experience, a professional financial planner is whom you should seek out for your coach. Your coach must be a person who truly gets what you're trying to accomplish and has a rigorous process to guide you, track your progress and update your plan on a regular basis. You will need a financial fitness coach who will be there with you through the ups and downs of the investment cycle and as your career develops, so be aware of this when you look for your coach.

How do you find a reputable financial fitness coach? Perhaps the easiest approach is to type "financial planning" into a browser or, in Canada, go to www.IAFP.ca. Identify two or three potential candidates. Check consumer websites to see what others may have experienced. In other words, shop around—and once you've narrowed it down to a manageable number, interview the candidates and listen carefully to what they say. Do they have a process to capture what you are trying to achieve? Do they listen to you? Have they experienced longer-term investment cycles (10 years or more)? Do they have a client base that includes higher-net-worth families and families that are in retirement?

Here is a list of some traits you should look for and certain questions you should ask when interviewing a financial planner as part of the selection process.

First, is this planner a good *listener*? Did he or she encourage you to express your aspirations and goals prior to offering up advice? Beware of the advisor who starts by telling you what you need before you've told him or her what you want. Perhaps the best analogy is the sporting-goods salesperson who tries to sell you this brand of ski boot or that brand of skate—before measuring your foot.

Fit, be it in selecting ski boots, skates or the best financial products, is everything.

Second, does the planner make *big promises*? One advisor caught on hidden camera by the CBC told a young woman she could make "40 or 50 percent in a year." Then you should find another candidate. The old adage "If it sounds too good to be true, it probably is to good to be true" holds here.

Third, does the candidate planner ask you about your perception of risk?

Typically a younger person has a somewhat higher risk tolerance than individuals in their sixties or seventies simply because their time horizon is longer. But much depends on one's financial knowledge, experiences and goals. If you want to buy a house or condo in 10 years and/or retire in 40, you need a strategy that gets you there with a risk level that is appropriate and well understood.

Fourth, one way or another, financial advice does not come free. How effectively does your candidate planner explain his or her compensation model to you? A good planner will be up front about these topics. If the person is evasive, move on.

Let's say you now have chosen a financial planner, one who has listened to you and gets your situation and aspirations. What now?

Basically it is now your turn to listen. A good financial planner will do an assessment of your overall financial picture and will present you with several options to achieve your goals. Like any good coach, once you have developed a plan, he or she will establish a scheduled program make sure you are stay on track.

If this sounds a bit like a coach checking to see if you showed up for practice or did your assigned wind sprints or repetitions, well, it is. But most of us want that, and almost all of us need it!

CHAPTER 5A
A Rookie's Draft Sheet is a Net-Worth Statement

Much as a rookie's entire pre-draft career can be summarized into some statistics on a draft sheet, your financial strength can be summarized in *one* number. By simply subtracting everything you owe from everything you own, you will know your net worth. This should be a positive number, and it should grow each and every year. It is the ideal way to keep score of your finances and a very important way of tracking your progress, especially when it seems like you are not making any progress at all.

Case in point, let's say you have purchased an older condo at a great price, but you need to invest some money into renovations. The cost of the condo was $125,000, which you paid in cash. But you are now tapped out and your renovation costs will total about $24,000.

The going rate for a renovated condo is $160,000–170,000. You decide to go ahead with the renovation but have to finance the $24,000 through an equity line of credit (mortgage).

Once done, you owe $24,000 and have decided to pay this off over 36 months at $8000/year plus interest.

On the surface, you feel poorer. You have less cash available per month, and you now owe $24,000 on a condo that you were living in free and clear.

By calculating your net worth number, however, will will see a very different picture.

Your financial planner commends you on your decision to renovate because your net worth has now increased.

Calculated as follows:

	Prerenovations	Postrenovations
Condo Value	$125k	$160k
Debt (mortgage)	$0	($24k)
Net worth	$125k	$136k

If you were to sell all your condo and pay off debt post-renovation, you will have added $11k to your net worth. In sports speak, your playing value has just increased significantly, and many more teams will be interested in acquiring a player with your talent!

CHAPTER SIX

The Mentor

What, exactly, is a mentor? How does this individual differ from a financial advisor?

A good mentor is someone with greater experience than you, an individual who has not only achieved success professionally and personally but is willing to share these experiences, both positive and negative.

This could be a family member, a parent, grandparent, or an uncle or aunt. Or it could be a close family friend. It could also be someone at your place of work. Oftentimes successful individuals in business, the Professionals or artists are quite willing—and flattered—to be asked to mentor a younger person. This can be especially true of people who are in senior positions. They tend to be less focused on climbing the ladder of success (because they're already at the top rung) and much more open to sharing their insights.

Again, what you are looking for is a good two-way conversation, one where both parties listen to the other.

For example, a mentor who blabs on about their own experiences without linking them to practical advice in the here and now isn't really a mentor—this person is too self absorbed!

A good mentor should be inspirational to you, someone who has demonstrated by their actions and results, successes you respect and can relate to. A good mentor will have character traits you respect and is possibly someone who has had the benefit of experience through failures and successes in life, where failures were looked at simply as setbacks and not taken personally.

Failures in finances, just like setbacks in sports, must be overcome with reflection and adjustments and always with a positive focus—not by giving up!

Organizations in various sectors, such as finance, technology, pharmaceutical and retail have formal mentoring programs allowing employees from diverse backgrounds or working in a specific industry sectors like investment banking, retail or finance, to support one another in a mentorship-like role. In sports and in personal finance, learning by example can be a highly effective way to progress.

In some organizations, options to find a mentor may be more limited and less formalized. This might mean you will need look outside your own organization to another, similar company or firm for mentorship. A university alumni office is also a good resource—many will pair up senior alumni with recent grads. If you are a recent immigrant or first- or second-generation Canadian, you might wish to consider looking to a cultural centre or heritage organization for suggestions.

In all instances, it is in your responsibility to seek out a good mentor, so take the initiative.

It is worth exploring what is available and selecting a path that makes the most sense for your individual needs. Nearly every company has a veteran or two—a Derek Jeter or a Big Papi (baseball player David Américo Ortiz Arias)—who are willing and capable of providing advice and valuable career counselling. Most successful people, whatever their field of endeavour, would welcome a chance to encourage your success.

Once you choose your coach and your mentor, be "coachable." Listen to what they say and do the "exercises" they prescribe. *Try not to over-question or be too critical.* If you have chosen your mentors well, their suggestions will have been well thought out, tried, tested and true.

With a good coach, your financial planner and a good mentor, you now have a team to get you off to the right start as a rookie and before you know it, you'll slip into veteran status.

CHAPTER SEVEN

The Veteran

In a few years you begin to hit your stride. You have built up enough experience and acquired sufficient skills to have moved past the dreaded "rookie" tag that prospective employers put on those with fewer than three years' experience in the workforce.

More importantly you have likely been slotted into the lineup as a valued contributor to the success of the team. With any luck, your salary has progressed and you have been rewarded for your efforts with annual performance-based bonuses and well-deserved promotions.

In short, you have become an integral part of the team, the organization or you own enterprise. Assuming you have been listening to your coach and/or mentor, you have begun to accumulate significant savings. If you have hit the 30 percent suggested savings mark, after two years you could have anywhere from $30,000 to $50,000 saved, invested and growing.

It is at this point that you may begin to see money differently.

You may also start to see a notable difference between your approach to money and that of your friends'—because you will actually have some!

By creating and then sticking to a plan your approach will begin to reap visible rewards.

This should lead to a number of emotional benefits—a feeling of being more secure, more empowered and freer to make more and better choices in your life. In short, you are becoming the master of your own destiny.

You should feel very proud of your achievements. This combination of strong emotional feedback and tangible financial reward should act as a powerful incentive to continue on your path. In just two or three years of executing your plan, you will not only improve your financial life but your whole approach to life.

Good versus Bad Debt

What might you do with these savings and your positive cash flow? Let's revisit the concept of debt. It is at this point, depending on your objectives and priorities, you might consider taking on "good debt."

What is good debt?

Good debt is used to acquire things that typically appreciate in value, such as houses, certain types of investments or perhaps a university education or masters degree.

Bad debt is money borrowed for things that usually depreciate in value, such as automobiles, vacations and luxury goods. In fact virtually any consumer good is likely to decline in value over time.

There is also what I call *really* bad debt, in the form of interest charged on the unpaid monthly balance on your credit card, and late payment fees. Not only are most purchases put on credit cards of the depreciating variety, but the interest rate charged on the unpaid balance can be upwards of 18 percent. Credit cards do have a convenience factor—few of us want to carry around big wads of cash—but if you are carrying any debt on these cards you're making a rookie mistake, unworthy of your veteran status.

The solution is to arrange your finances in such a way that you can pay off the full amount each month. Auto-pay options work well, but if you autopay, you should continue to review your statement in detail monthly. The devil is in the details here, and ignoring the responsibility of checking your restaurant bills, credit card and bank statements can lead to costly mistakes. In time you will want to consider talking to your bank about establishing a line of credit as a smarter alternative to credit card debt. This allows you the convenience of using the credit card for larger (long term) purchases, emergencies or "must-have" purchases, hopefully accumulating points on your card for travel or other luxuries coupled with the means to pay off the balance at the end of the month at an interest rate less than one third of what credit card companies charge. The important thing to remember here is that you *must* have a plan to pay off longer-term debt based on your cash flow, much as you have a plan to save regularly. In fact, they are one in the same plan.

Both debt reduction and savings will improve your net worth—similar to the +/- stat for a hockey player!

As for incurring debt for things that appreciate in value, your guide should be those goals and priorities you established back at the beginning—goals that you reflect on and update yearly as they are achieved and as your lifestyle evolves.

Just as any athlete has to undergo a physical checkup each year as he or she reports to training camp, it is critical that you take an inventory of your situation annually, and that includes an update of your personal goals for the year ahead. Don't just think about them—you *must* write them down. They must also be written down by *you*, not your advisor or mentor.

Why is it important to actually write out these goals?

I believe that writing down goals and objectives is an activity that psychologically creates a contract between your mind and your body. The physical act of writing to yourself clarifies what you wish to achieve and makes you accountable for getting it done. It also serves as a useful starting point when you meet with your financial planner or mentor. He or she needs to know what you see as your goals if this person is going to help you with a strategy to achieve them successfully.

Start by listing all the goals that are significant to you and then from that list create a list of the goals that you want to obtain in the near future. This will allow you to focus better. The process of goal setting (some refer to this as a dream board) will require you to put aside some time for serious quiet reflection with no distractions. Allow yourself to wander and picture your life in the future. Goal setting can and should include all the things that are important for you to achieve (not just your financial ambitions). Consider issues such as health, fitness, family, friends, relationships and more when you work on your list. I suggest you schedule quarterly time on your calendar to review your list and your progress.

This is a process I have found most effective. I continue to goal set quarterly and plan to do this every year for the rest of my life. I hope that if you do this, you will be pleasantly surprised by what you can achieve, and this feeling will inspire you to continue this process as you follow your progress and achievements.

I have added a worksheet at the end of this chapter to help you on your journey. Allow yourself some quiet time to reflect on your life goals and write them down.

CHAPTER EIGHT

Investing Like a Pro

You might think that this chapter contains the key to your ultimate financial wealth. In fact, over a lifetime, not making amateur mistakes has been proven to increase investor returns by up to 3.5 percent on average/year and this is significant. At retirement where savings accumulated can be in the millions of dollars, 3% per million is $30,000 per year saved by not making amateur investment mistakes.

That is a significant performance gain! Consider the advantage you will have if these mistakes are avoided over the 30+ year accumulation stage.

This is when planning and coaching have a major impact on your ability to see your goals through to a successful ending. If you goal is to grow your net worth (akin to improving your skills as a player), then there are three fundamental steps that should be followed.

The first step is to learn how to save. This is comparable to the commitment a professional athlete must have to a regular training discipline so he or she performs at the highest level.

The second step is to understand your timelines and to structure your investing accordingly. This matches closely the training regime a marathoner or an Olympic athlete must have to peak during the event (which could be once every four years for the Olympic athlete).

Step three is to learn how *not to be* discouraged by setbacks. Injuries and game losses can be a real mind game for athletes. For investors, market corrections and economic recessions can be the same. Those of us who do not have the benefit of a mentor or coach to calm emotions can often make impulsive decisions that seriously impact their long-term plans (e.g., selling or buying at the wrong time). These are strong emotions to overcome as they play on our fight-or-flight responses. These are responses that have evolved from our survival behaviour through evolution.

Step one can come from personal drive, but step two is greatly enhanced with coaches, trainers, nutritionists, physiotherapists and other professionals who have studied the sport you are training for.

For the "sport" of finance, step two would benefit from a financial planner and an investment coach or advisor. I am talking about experience here. The goal when investing should be to match your timeline with investments that you can continue to accumulate. The investments must be tax efficient. This will take knowledge and skills that you may not have at this point on your journey.

Market Corrections Favour the Rookie!

It seems to me that the investing world is the only place where people are motivated to buy things that are overvalued because they have gone up in price and to sell things that are undervalued because they are dropping in price. Compare this to our obsession with finding gas a few cents cheaper, driving out of our way to tank up to save a couple of cents per litre. The amateur investor would do just the opposite.

What they do in the investing world would be the equivalent to buying gas at a station that has just posted a price increase without comparing this to other stations in the area, on their simple assumption that gas prices at all stations are on the rise—so better to buy it now. This phenomenon is classic human behaviour. We tend to think in patterns. The media plays on this behaviour either knowingly or unknowingly (the stories are written by reporters who are themselves subjected to the same behaviour). The idea that because oil prices are trending down they will continue to go down or that because gold prices are up, they will continue to go up makes for an easy emotional leap, but rarely does it reflect reality.

Watch the news stories when the Canadian dollar is declining against the US dollar or when the weather has trended warmer for a period of time. Invariably you will read that the trend will continue. Does this ever play out? Check the stories a few months later, and I think you will find that there often is no pattern at all. It is an easy emotional leap to see short-term adjustments as trends that will continue in the same direction—it is how we are wired.

All-star athletes have learned that streaks and droughts begin and end. They will most likely have surrounded themselves with talented coaches to keep them mentally and physically on track. It is rare to see a professional athlete compete at the highest level who is totally self-taught and self-motivated. It is just too difficult to master all the emotions and physical demands of staying competitive at the highest level on your own.

Having confidence in what you own and who advises you is key to making good decisions in challenging times.

So to understand how market corrections favour the rookie, you first have to be confident that what you are invested in has value and that the investments are not speculative, trendy or based on rumours or tips.

Let me explain why this is so.

Let's assume you want to buy a house, so you pick a great neighbourhood and find a house that is not the most expensive one on the street, and it is priced fairly. In the housing market on any given month prices may be higher or lower, but you should be reasonably confident that the house has value and will be priced appropriately because you did your homework and understand the housing market. After all, you have to live somewhere.

Let's compare this to an imaginary twin who, faced with the same decision, wants to go big. He or she buys a great house in a below-average neighbourhood and pays less than you but buys the largest house on the street, paying full asking price. If the housing market corrects this property, will likely see a much greater drop in value for a much longer period of time than yours. Why? Because there are many factors at play when pricing is set. Location, relative value and demand all factor into the price.

Now what if your investment model was to buy one property per year every year? During a market correction you pick up the same house for 25 percent less. Would you really be concerned that your money was at risk knowing you will be holding onto this asset through the market cycle?

Most probably you would look forward to these market corrections, as they would be great opportunities to pick up investment properties at below market prices. Life insurance companies do this regularly as they invest their "float" (money in reserve to pay out claims) because their holding period before they must pay a claim can be 50 years or more.

Your twin may not be so convinced. His or her house dropped in value by much more than 25 percent and will take many more years to return to the original purchase price.

With good investments and a regular purchasing plan, market corrections definitely favour the rookie who is saving.

Steady Hands Win This Race

You can have excellent coaching at a very reasonable cost to become an all-star investor. The decision to surround yourself with coaching talent can be a huge multiplier in the growth of your net worth.

Why is this so? I think that there are two main reasons for this: suitability and emotional support.

Excellent planners/advisors will make sure your investments match your goals. They will help you through challenging economic times with experienced advice. They have more likely been exposed to full market cycles than you and can make more rational decisions because their experience will keep their emotions in check. They are obligated (by in-clients' best interest rules) to adjust your investment strategy to your changing financial or economic circumstances. This is very hard to do without a support team.

Brokers, ETFs, Managed Money

You may have heard about these investment choices.

The subject of investment styles is highly complex and can be very opinionated depending on whom you talk to or what you read. I can fill a book on the pros and cons of each investment style, but for the purposes of this book PILOT 1, I would like to stick to what I consider the basics.

Brokers are licensed to sell individual stocks and bonds, mutual funds and options. If they are not acting on your instructions, they could be considered portfolio managers (although many licensed brokers use mutual funds extensively to build portfolios which are managed by other portfolio managers).

ETF's (exchange traded funds) are basically a collection of stocks or fund of stocks built by filtering (by computer) the stock exchange indexes or listings. They have been described as the future of portfolio construction. They are or can be low cost because they are run by computer and either filter from or track stock markets or indexes already created.

Managed money has been labelled as expensive and perhaps unnecessary in today's computer-engineered low-cost world. Managed money refers to the process portfolio managers use to create pools of stocks, bonds and other investment products that require computer analysis, filtering and the human analysis for final decision-making on what to hold and when to sell.

What about "do-it-yourselfers"?

They are investors who build their own investment funds from stocks, options and mutual funds. They will need to use a broker or discount broker to do this so, let's group them with brokers for investment-style purposes.

The good:

Both ETFs and managed money make decisions to buy and sell the investments that they hold on your behalf at the fund level. You will not be receiving a phone call from your broker asking you if you want to buy or sell a given stock, forcing you into a decision-making process where you have insufficient knowledge and probably little interest, which can cause much anxiety.

Disclaimer: Some brokerage accounts are called discretionary, which means you give your broker the right to buy and sell on your behalf without requesting consent for each transaction. Let's lump this into the category of managed money for obvious reasons.

The not-so-good:

Brokers of nondiscretionary accounts are basically portfolio managers without a public record and with arguably limited resources to make transactions for all their clients at an appropriate time.

For example, you are one of 250 clients and your account is somewhere in the middle investment size. When your broker decides it's time to sell some bank stocks, do you think you will get the call first, or will you be call 150? How long will it take before your broker works down the list from largest client to smallest client to get to you? Will you be available to take that call, and if you're available, will you agree with the decision to sell?

These factors can negatively impact your returns over time.

ETFs:

The original ETF model that simply tracked an index was in many ways a voting machine. Most indexes use capitalization (stock price times the number of stocks issued) as their calculator for determining what stock is included in the index. The index is recalculated once per year. As a result, many stocks in these indexes have what I call a growth bias. This means they would be included if the investing public really bid up the stock price often regardless of traditional factors such as profitability, market share and management team.

This can lead to really big drops in value during market corrections. (Look up the information technology bubble [dot-com bubble] of the year 2000 for more some examples.

Today the ETF market has completely evolved with what are called hybrid products. These ETFs use computer filters and sometimes a managerial-level review to create subgroups of companies with certain characteristics. These reviews are generally once per year but can occur more often.

As the manager overview and frequency of reviews increase, so does the cost of these products. It would also not be a stretch to say that ETFs are not forward looking investments, they generally look at past results to make buy sell decisions.

The reason:

Most studies I have read and my experience with my clients' portfolios have confirmed that asset mix plays a significant role in investment returns. Asset mix is the blend of different types of investments that make up a portfolio. We are talking north of 90 percent of all returns are dependant on asset mix.

If you own the Canadian financial services sector in an ETF, mutual fund or through a broker and this sector is growing, as long as you hold a broad selection of stocks (let's assume 10 or more in this sector), all three investments will see growth. But if your investment choices are so specific that you do not own this sector you can miss up to 90 percent of total investment returns in a given year. When I say investment returns, I mean both positive and negative. It does not matter at all if US small cap stocks are in demand and go on a tear if you don't own any. Since most ETFs and many mutual funds are sector specific, who is going to make the decision on which sector to own and when to sell or reduce your weighting in a sector?

So now that we have some broad definitions of investment styles what is the right choice for the "net worth investor," who is interested in continuously growing his or her net worth over their lifetyme?

The answer is of course, "it depends". In my experience, the first and most important role that must be filled is that of asset manager. Your financial planner can provide that skill or hire that skill out through an investment-management company, a financial advisor or a broker. In all cases a specialist should be hired to provide that skill.

The investment decisions that follow should depend on where the market is in its cycle. In my analysis, a market that has recently corrected will generally see growth or recovery across a broad spectrum of companies, so an ETF might be a good low-cost choice here. But in a mature market with high valuations some individual stock analysis may be required to pick out individual companies that are growing and to protect you from overvalued stock shocks especially during major market corrections.

This will require the technical analysis, skill and judgment of an active manager.

As you can imagine, a given investment portfolio that participates in many different markets can benefit from both styles of investing. In my experience, the choices are best left to a professional asset manager who should be chosen based on his or her track record, access to research information and perhaps with the guidance of your mentor.

In all cases, learn to be patient and well diversified, and above all, maintain your commitment to regular savings.

To assist you with the task of finding appropriate financial guidance, I have found a document (courtesy of CI Investments/the value of advice) that lists *50 ways financial advisors/planners can support you* to be most valuable. I encourage you to refer to these questions to evaluate and choose appropriate financial planning advice.

When seeking financial advice, a financial-planning professional should have these 50 characteristics and processes in place:

1. Being honest with you, appreciating and valuing you
2. Caring about you and your money more than anyone who does not share your surname
3. Being someone you can trust and get advice from for all your financial matters
4. Understanding what money means to you and what motivates you
5. Listening and asking questions to help you identify and articulate your needs, goals and objectives
6. Working with you to alleviate worries that keep you awake at night
7. Coaching you to do the things that will help accomplish your goals

8. Monitoring changes in your life and family situation

9. Guiding you through difficult periods in the stock market by sharing a historical perspective

10. Acting as a sounding/discussion board for ideas you are considering

11. Providing guidance on what course you should take and giving you an objective perspective

12. Anticipating future changes and proactively working through them with you

13. Keeping you on track

14. Helping you make important financial-related decisions

15. Helping organize and prioritize your financial life

16. Helping you determine where you are at present

17. Helping you formalize realistic goals and put them in writing

18. Making specific recommendations to help you meet your goals

19. Establishing a clear strategy and action plan

20. Suggesting creative alternatives that you may not have considered

21. Preparing an investment policy statement for you

22. Reviewing and recommending life insurance policies to protect your family

23. Staying up-to-date on tax law changes

24. Helping you reduce your taxes by reviewing your tax returns for possible savings

25. Working with your tax and legal advisors and other professionals to facilitate and coordinate your overall financial plans

26. Identifying your savings shortfalls

27. Helping establish your will and estate, retirement and business succession plans

28. Helping you transfer wealth efficiently to the next generation

29. Developing and monitoring a strategy for debt reduction

30. Preparing an asset-allocation strategy for you to diversify your investments and achieve the best rate of return for your level of risk tolerance

31. Performing due diligence on money managers and mutual fund managers to ensure appropriate investment recommendations

32. Staying up-to-date on changes in the investment world

33. Reviewing and revising your portfolio as conditions change

34. Helping consolidate, simplify and improve your investment performance

35. Monitoring and managing your investments and converting them into income as needed

36. Helping you establish better planning and record keeping

37. Exploring and reviewing potential income-splitting and tax-minimization strategies with you

38. Recommending and completing appropriate tax-loss selling solutions

39. Repositioning investments to take full advantage of tax rules

40. Providing full disclosure and transparency on their fees and processes

41. Proactively keeping in touch with you by providing customized and personalized information

42. Providing referrals to and liaising with other professionals such as accountants, actuaries and tax lawyers as needed

43. Being only a telephone call away to answer financial questions for you

44. Serving as a human glossary of financial terms such as beta, P/E ratio and Sharpe ratio

45. Listening and providing feedback in a way that a magazine or newsletter writer cannot

46. Helping educate your children and grandchildren about investments and financial concepts

47. Educating you on retirement, savings and other financial topics

48. Helping with other non-financial advice
49. Providing easy-to-read account statements and reports
50. Holding seminars to educate you on significant and/or new financial concepts

CHAPTER NINE

The All-Star Hall of Fame

It may have been challenging, but I hope you can say your career has been successful beyond your wildest dreams.

If you're an athlete, you might be only be 35 or so. If your sport is in the working world, you may be in your 50s or 60s. If you are extremely successful, you might even be in your 40s.

Statistically, it would be reasonable to say you may still have another 25, 30 or possibly even 40 years of healthy living ahead of you.

Discounting the financial support government pensions will provide (because it is based on a very low threshold of income), I expect you have cultivated and grown your net worth to the point that it can support your cash-flow needs in retirement. By taking financial matters into your own hands and starting out from your rookie income, you sought out advice, chose a mentor and a financial planner, exercised intelligent discipline in spending and began to save for your future at a young age.

After years of market experiences both positive and negative, you've realized there is really no other way. Everyone has an opportunity to grow his or her net worth in his or her lifetime, and everyone is subject to the same variables, income, lifestyle, markets and emotions, to name a few.

I expect you now have a meaningful net worth in the many millions of dollars and can afford to live comfortably in your own unique way.

What made you so lucky?

Hopefully this book will help you with the basic choices you can make to turn a rookie career into an all-star career. As an all-star living from your investments, new and often different choices must be made to make this period of your life more secure.

The reason for this is that you will likely have to withdraw money every year from your investments to maintain your lifestyle. This can be done quite effectively with guidance and well structured investments.

The decisions that have to be made in future stages of your life will lead quite nicely into the subjects of book 2 or "PILOT 2" Financial Fitness for life.

The four rules for success:

1- Do what you say you will do.

2- Finish what you start.

3- Be on time.

4- Show your appreciation.

Your Personal Goals List

1

2

3

4

5

6

7

8

9

10